The Historic Codfish

Also from Westphalia Press

westphaliapress.org

The Historic Codfish

A History of the Emblem of the Codfish in the Hall of the House of Representatives

by George H. Proctor
Samuel D. Hildreth
Wm. Frank Parsons

WESTPHALIA PRESS
An imprint of Policy Studies Organization

Westphalia Press
An imprint of Policy Studies Organization
1527 New Hampshire Ave., NW
Washington, D.C. 20036
dgutierrezs@ipsonet.org

ISBN-13: 978-1935907817
ISBN-10: 1935907816

Cover design by Taillefer Long at Illuminated Stories:
www.illuminatedstories.com

Updated material and comments on this edition
can be found at the Westphalia Press website:
www.westphaliapress.org

A HISTORY

OF THE

EMBLEM OF THE CODFISH

IN THE

Hall of the House of Representatives.

COMPILED BY A COMMITTEE OF THE HOUSE.

" No sea but what is vexed by their fisheries, no climate that is not witness to their toils." — EDMUND BURKE.

BOSTON:
WRIGHT AND POTTER PRINTING CO., STATE PRINTERS,
18 POST OFFICE SQUARE.
1895.

PREFACE.

The committee having in charge the compilation of the history of the codfish, being unable to incorporate in the work the action of the Legislature subsequent to the filing of their report, deemed it best not to chronicle therein any of the proceedings of the present year, but to summarize briefly the several acts and resolves and present them as an introduction, thus furnishing in one work all that appears of record concerning this historical emblem.

The members-elect of the House of Representatives for the year 1895 assembled in the accustomed chamber in the "Bulfinch front" January 2 and organized. The House was to meet on the following day in the new chamber, in the State House extension.

The question of taking with it the "representation of a codfish," which for more than a hundred years had never missed a "roll call," was brought up for consideration. It was, however, deemed wise to investigate the significance of

the emblem before its removal, to which end the
following order, on motion of Representative
Ernest W. Roberts of Chelsea, was unanimously
adopted : —

Ordered, That a committee of three be appointed to
prepare and report to the House the complete history of
the codfish suspended in the chamber of the House of
Representatives.

It may be of interest to note that this was the
last business transacted in the old chamber. On
Thursday, January 10, Representatives Ernest W.
Roberts of Chelsea, Richard W. Irwin of Northampton and James A. Gallivan of Boston were
appointed the committee to prepare the history.
After nearly two months of painstaking research
and investigation their report was submitted to
the House, and on Monday, March 4, the following order was offered by Mr. Woodfall of
Rockport :—

Ordered, That the Sergeant-at-Arms be and is hereby
directed to cause the immediate removal of the ancient
"representation of a codfish" from its present position
in the chamber recently vacated by the House, and to
cause it to be suspended in a suitable place over the

Speaker's chair in this chamber, in order that the House of 1895 may further the intent and purpose of the House of 1784, wherein it voted to "hang the representation of a codfish in the room where the House sit, as a memorial of the importance of the cod fishery to the welfare of this Commonwealth, as had been usual formerly;" and that a committee of fifteen members accompany the Sergeant-at-Arms when said memorial is transferred to this chamber.

Consideration of this order was, on motion of the same gentleman, postponed until March 7, and specially assigned for half-past two o'clock P.M., at which time it was debated at length.

Mr. Brown of Gloucester, during the debate, presented the following resolutions, and asked unanimous consent that they be entered in the Journal of the House. There being no objection, the request was granted: —

To the Honorable House of Representatives.

Whereas, The question of the removal of the old codfish, so many years a feature of the House of Representatives, is being considered in our State Legislature; and

Whereas, The city of Gloucester having from the earliest settlement been prominently identified with the fishing industry, which was prosecuted previous to the Revolution so successfully as to make Gloucester the second town in size in the county of Essex at that time, and has since so increased as to make this city the largest fishing port in the country ; therefore

Resolved, That the Business Men's Association of the City of Gloucester desire to place themselves on record as favoring the retention of this ancient emblem of our industry, which is so interwoven into the prosperity of our old Commonwealth from its earliest history, and as a testimonial to the sterling qualities of the pioneers whose labors builded so firmly the foundations on which rest so firmly the stability of our institutions.

To those familiar with the history and development of Massachusetts there is nothing about the State House more interesting or more suggestive than this codfish. It tells of commerce, war, diplomacy ; of victories won by Massachusetts. It symbolizes the sources of our original wealth ; the nursery of those mariners who manned the gun-decks of our frigates ; our issues and struggles with England.

The number of pounds of codfish landed at the port of Gloucester during the year 1894 was 43,000,000. In addition, 10,000,000 pounds were also landed by her fleets at other ports, making a total in round numbers of 53,000,000 pounds of this valuable fish product wrested from old ocean by the hardy Gloucester fishermen in a single year.

GEORGE H. PROCTOR,
SAMUEL D. HILDRETH,
WM. FRANK PARSONS,
Committee.

GLOUCESTER, Jan. 17, 1895.

After debate, the previous question having been ordered, on motion of Mr. Grover of Canton, the order was adopted, and the Speaker appointed the following members as the committee: Messrs. Woodfall of Rockport, Tarr of Gloucester, Gauss of Salem, Wadden of Marblehead, Brown of Gloucester, Jordan of Salem, Foss of Cottage City, Russell of Salem, Cook of Provincetown, Irwin of Northampton, Roberts of Chelsea, Gallivan of Boston, Bullock of Manchester, Stocker of Beverly and Gardner of Nantucket.

The committee immediately proceeded, under the escort of Sergeant-at-Arms J. G. B. Adams, to the discharge of its duty. Upon arriving at the chamber of the old House of Representatives, the emblem was lowered from its abiding place by John Kinnear, assistant doorkeeper of the House, wrapped in the American flag, deposited upon a bier, and borne to the House of Representatives by Messengers Edwin Gould, T. F. Pedrick, Frank Wilson and Sidney Gardner. As the procession entered the House the members arose, the historic emblem was received with a vigorous round of applause, and was deposited upon a table in front of the Speaker's desk.

Thereupon the committee appointed to compile the complete history of the codfish suspended in the chamber of the House of Representatives submitted their report, which was read by Messrs. Roberts and Gallivan, and Mr. Irwin delivered the address herein contained.

The same day Mr. Gauss of Salem introduced on leave a Resolve providing for the publication of the report of the committee, together with the speech of Mr. Irwin.

Mr. Roberts of Chelsea also introduced a Resolve providing for the painting of the representation of the codfish and suspending the same in the chamber of the House of Representatives, to be done under the direction of the Speaker of the House. Both of these resolves were adopted March 12 and referred to the committee on Finance.

On March 25 the resolves were reported from the committee on Finance "ought to pass," and were adopted.

Monday, April 29, the following order, offered by Mr. Roe of Worcester, was adopted: —

Ordered, That the historic figure of the codfish, when suspended, be placed opposite the Speaker's chair, between the two sets of central columns, and under the names " Motley " and " Parkman."

The emblem was painted by Mr. Walter M. Brackett of Boston, a well-known and talented artist, and was suspended in its present position May 6.

ERNEST W. ROBERTS.
RICHARD W. IRWIN.
JAMES A. GALLIVAN.

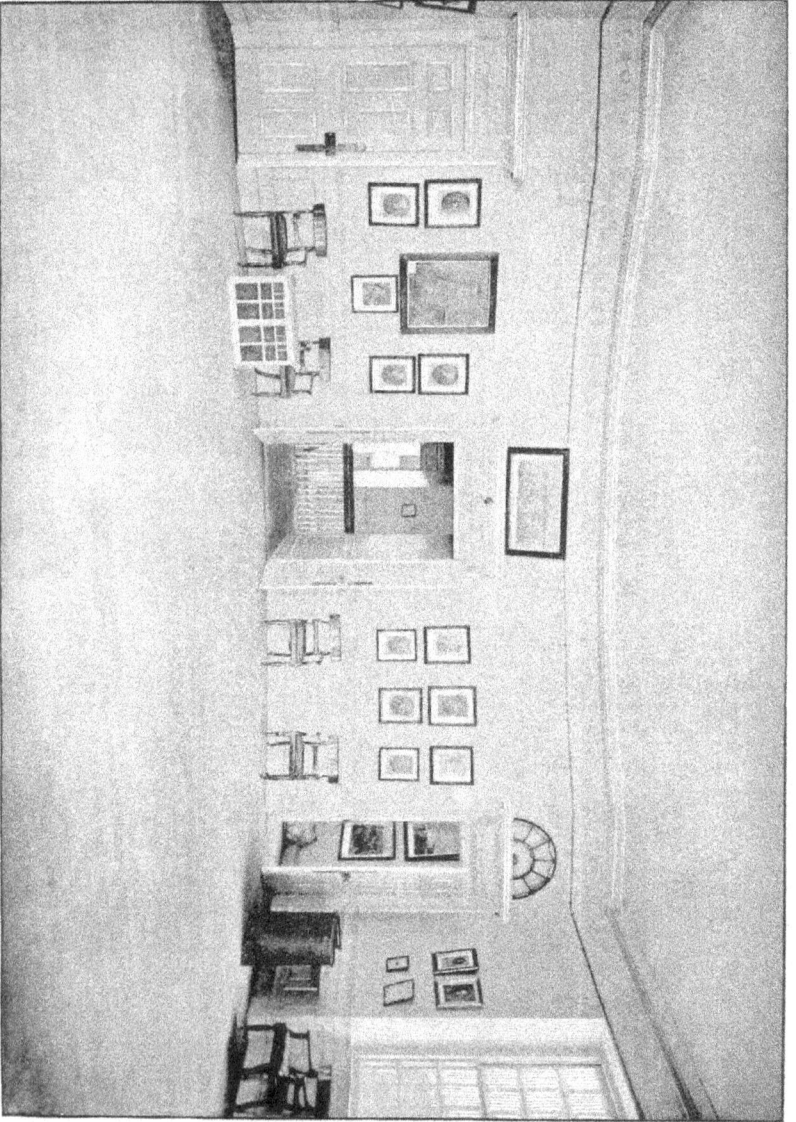

REPRESENTATIVES' CHAMBER, OLD STATE HOUSE.

Report of the Committee.

Commonwealth of Massachusetts.

House of Representatives, March 7, 1895.

The committee appointed to prepare a history of the emblem of the codfish submit the following report: —

ERNEST W. ROBERTS,
RICHARD W. IRWIN,
JAMES A. GALLIVAN,
The Committee.

House of Representatives, March 7, 1895.

Accepted: EDWARD A. MCLAUGHLIN,
Clerk.

CHAPTER I.

Poised high aloft in the old hall of the Massachusetts House of Representatives, riding serenely the sound waves of debate, unperturbed by the ebb and flow of enactment and repeal or the desultory storms that vexed the nether depths of oratory, there has hung through immemorial years an ancient codfish, quaintly wrought in wood and painted to the life.

Humble the subject and homely the design; yet this painted image bears on its finny front a majesty greater than the dignity that art can lend to graven gold or chiselled marble. The sphere it fills is vaster than that through which its prototype careered with all the myriad tribes of the great deep. The lessons that may be learned of it are nobler than any to be drawn from what is only beautiful; for this sedate and solitary fish is instinct with memories and prophecy, like an oracle. It swims symbolic in that wider sea whose confines are the limits set to the activities of human thought. It typifies to the citizens of the Commonwealth and of the world the founding of a State. It commemorates Democracy. It celebrates the rise of free institutions. It emphasizes progress. It epitomizes Massachusetts.

To the sober student of the world's past this historic codfish is fraught with ripe significance. A few details as to the origin and vicissitudes of this material emblem may shed some light on its serious purpose and high mission.

This old codfish has kept its place under all administrations, and has looked upon outgoing and incoming legislative assemblies, for more than one hundred years. It does not appear under what precise circumstances this familiar representation assumed its position; but it is an assured fact that the identical image which hangs to-day in the hall recently occupied by the lower branch of the Great and General Court came there from the old State House at the head of State Street, when the archives were transferred in 1798. That it was suspended in the old State House since 1784 appears from the following entry in the Journal of the House of Representatives of Wednesday, March 17, 1784: —

"Mr. Rowe moved the House that leave might be given to hang up the representation of a Cod Fish in the room where the House sit, as a memorial of the importance of the Cod-Fishery to the welfare of this Commonwealth, as had been usual formerly. The said motion having been seconded, the question was put, and leave given for the purpose aforesaid."

And so the emblem was suspended, and, as Mr. Rowe was a man of peculiar public spirit and patriotism, it is probable that he paid for the carving of the fish and all the expenses incident thereto, even those connected with its "hanging up in the room where the House sit," out of his own pocket.

It seems proper that something more than a mere reference should be made to the person to whose forethought and patriotism we owe the placing in our halls of legislation of so significant a reminder of an industry once the greatest in Massachusetts. It has been said of him he was "as true a friend to his country as any whose names have reached a greater renown." John, son of Joseph and Mary Rowe, was born at Exeter, Devon, England, on Nov. 16, 1715. The date of his departure from England is as unknown as that of his advent in Boston. That it was in his early youth is evident, for it is known that in 1740 he was made a member of St. John's Lodge of Freemasons, the first body of that fraternity to be established in

Boston, and the records show that he was then twenty-five years of age. That he took a deep and lasting interest in Masonry is shown by the fact that he was elected master of the lodge nine years later, being the fifth Provincial Grand Master of Masons in the year 1768. He held the office until his death. He made numerous investments in and about Boston, where he became the owner of considerable property, including the present Rowe's wharf, a residence on Pond, now Bedford, Street, and an estate in Milton. Chauncy Street for many years bore his name.

From the very beginning John Rowe was an active and earnest participant in the struggle of the colonists to free themselves from the tyrannies of the mother country. He was one of the fifty most prominent and influential merchants and business men of Boston who, on Dec. 19, 1760, signed a petition to the General Court charging the officers of the Crown with appropriating to their own use money belonging to the Province. All through the agitation aroused by the odious stamp acts he was an indefatigable worker for the repeal of those iniquitous laws. So active was he in this direction that one historian has credited him with leading the mob against the house of Lieutenant-Governor Hutchinson during the riots of 1765, caused by the enforcement of the stamp acts; although in justice to John Rowe it should be said that Hutchinson himself, in his account of this riot, states that the mob was led by one Mackintosh. John Rowe enjoyed in the highest degree the confidence and esteem of his

John Rowe

fellow citizens, and was repeatedly appointed on committees in town meetings. In 1764 he was so appointed one of a committee of five to inform the Rev. Mr. George Whitefield of a unanimous vote of thanks for the great service rendered by the reverend gentleman in raising money to relieve the distress occasioned by the disastrous fire of 1760, which caused so much suffering to the people of Boston. If not a leader and moving spirit among the Sons of Liberty, he was at least in close sympathy with them and their aims, for on May 6, 1766, that organization controlled the election of the Representatives to the General Court from Boston, and chose James Otis, Thomas Cushing, Samuel Adams, John Hancock and John Rowe, the latter being selected upon the motion of Samuel Adams; and the distinguished company in which he found himself was of itself ample evidence of his ability and standing in the community. Nor was this the only public office held by him, for on March 14 of the following year we find him elected one of the selectmen, having for colleagues John Hancock, Samuel Sewall, William Phillips and others but little less renowned. He held this office until 1769, when he declined a re-election, and the board thereupon unanimously extended him a vote of thanks for his past services. At this time he was also one of the firewards of the town.

Although now past middle age, his interest in public questions was as keen as ever, and his patriotism as ardent as in the days of the stamp act excitement; and four years later, in 1773, at the age of fifty-eight, we find him, in conjunction with Samuel Adams and Hancock, a leading spirit in the stirring scenes that led up to the famous "Boston Tea Party." It is claimed he was part owner in one of the vessels which brought to Boston the tea thrown into the harbor on the evening of Thursday, December 16; and from certain passages in his journal, covering the period from September, 1764, to July, 1779, it would seem the vessel was the "Eleanor," Captain Bruce. An entry in this journal, "I would Rather have Lost five hundred Guineas than Captain Bruce should have taken any of this Tea on board his Ship," indicates his annoyance that his vessel should have been implicated in this obnoxious proceeding; but self-interest did not deter him from doing all in his power to prevent the landing of the tea. The afternoon of Dec. 16, 1773, saw the Old South Church packed as it never had been before. At three o'clock it was estimated there were seven thousand people in and around the edifice. Samuel Adams, John Rowe, Young, Quincy and other distinguished citizens were upon the platform, exhorting the people to stand firm, and cautioning them to moderation. In the course of his address Rowe said, "Who knows how tea will mingle with salt water?"—a suggestion which was received with loud applause, and has been thought by many to be a foreshadowing of what was to take place if permission was not given the vessels to sail without landing their obnoxious cargo. Rowe and Hancock have been accredited with taking part in throwing the tea overboard; but it is almost certain the former had no actual hand in so doing, for he was still upon the platform when, a little after six o'clock, the "Mohawks" rushed by the church on their way to Griffin's wharf, where the ships were moored.

In 1743 John Rowe married Hannah Speakman in Boston. He was of a deeply religious turn of mind, and for many years was a member of the old Trinity Church, of which he was a warden from 1769 until 1777, and upon his death, Feb. 21, 1787, he was buried under the church.

There is a dim tradition that in the primitive House of Assembly of the Province there hung a codfish which was the gift of Judge Samuel Sewall, author of the famous "Diary." Judge Sewall died in 1729. His published remains make no mention of this traditional fish, and it is difficult to imagine that a man of his loquacious verbosity would have omitted to chronicle his munificence, either in his diary or his letters.

The expression, "as had been usual formerly," in the original motion of Mr. Rowe, apparently refers to this prehistoric creature of tradition, which hung in the old State, or Town, House. When this structure was burned, Dec. 9, 1747, the codfish doubtless went up in a whirl of smoke which still clouds its history to the peering vision of the antiquarian. The new Old State House (which stands to this day at the head of State Street) was erected in the succeeding year; and, at whatsoever date the old-time emblem was restored to its original place of honor, it is clear that it flourished there in all its pristine glory as early as 1773; for, in

an old bill of that year, presented by Thos. Crafts,
Jr., to the Province of Massachusetts Bay, for painting the State House, and which, from all that can be
learned, has not been disputed, appears the item : —

To painting Codfish, .   .   .   15 Shillings.

At some indeterminate time subsequent to the painting of the codfish by Thomas Crafts, Jr., it disappeared
from the State House and was doubtless destroyed, for
the closest historical research fails to shed any light
upon the time, manner or cause of its disappearance,
or to disclose any further reference to it whatever.
Mayhap some burly British trooper, quartered in the
improvised barracks of the old State House, took um-
brage at the spick and span elegance of the newly
painted emblem of colonial independence and thrift.
Such a one may have torn the cherished symbol from
the wall whence it had offered aid and comfort to the
rebel patriots, with its assurance of the material wealth
accessible to the embryonic State, and, in the spirit of
vandalism so prevalent at that age, used it to replenish
his evening camp fire. Whatever may have been its
fate in that epoch of political upheaval, no record was
left to tell the tale

There seems good reason to believe that this missing
fish, or its successor, which has come down to us, was
carved by one John Welch, a Boston patriot. Welch
was born Aug. 11, 1711. He was a well-known citi-
zen, and lived on Green Lane in West Boston. In
1756 he was a captain in the Ancient and Honorable

Artillery Company. He, too, was one of the signers of the famous petition or memorial, charging the officers of the Crown with appropriating to their own use money belonging to the Province. The descendants of John Welch have always insisted that he carved the State House codfish of to-day. His great-great-grandson, Capt. Francis Welch, is now living in Brookline, at the age of eighty-six, and he has recently stated that the truth of this assertion has always been recognized among the family traditions. It has been handed down from father to son uncontradicted for at least three generations. Captain Welch's father repeatedly told him that he heard the story from the lips of his grandfather, and never expressed the least doubt in regard to it.

Conceding the authenticity of this tradition, a question remains as to which of the two codfishes was the handiwork of John Welch. Welch died Feb. 9, 1789; so that, if he carved the fish now in the State House, he must have been in his seventy-fourth year. This seems unlikely, whereas he might easily have wrought the codfish Thomas Crafts painted; and it is quite probable that, in the growing vagueness of domestic tradition, the identity of the two may have been confounded. In that chaotic revolutionary period which left to us no record of the loss or destruction of the object of Thomas Crafts' artistic attention, the Welch family may easily have lost trace of it, and have taken it for granted that the older emblem is the actual symbol of to-day.

It has been said by some one that the old codfish has never been taken down since it was first suspended in the then new State House in 1798; but Capt. Thomas Tucker, the venerable doorkeeper of the House, can tell another story. Within his own recollection the old emblem has twice been lowered, and he furthermore says that the codfish did not always occupy its present vantage ground. It used to hang from a point in the ceiling directly over the Speaker's desk, but in the fifties it was shifted to the rear of the chamber. In 1867, for a brief space, the fish was missing from its accustomed haunt; but it soon returned, brighter than before, in a new coat of submarine motley. Again, in 1874, while the chamber was being renovated, the codfish was taken down to be repainted; and at the time Captain Tucker measured it, finding its length to be four feet and eleven inches. He also noted that it was carved from a solid block of wood. Since that time, a period of twenty-one years, the sacred emblem has not been profaned by mortal touch.

CHAPTER II.

To the historian it seems quite natural that the codfish, an article of pure, plain, natural food, should be the emblem of the practical, frugal spirit which laid the foundation of Massachusetts. And, while the term "codfish aristocracy" is sometimes used as one of reproach, the reproach lies in the departure by their descendants from the simple ways of the early fishermen; and if by "codfish aristocracy" we should be understood to mean the living fisher-folk of Cape Ann and Cape Cod, then we have excellent reason for aiming to preserve such an aristocracy in honor.

"If Massachusetts ever had a tutelary genius among the brute creation, it was the codfish," wrote an essayist thirty years ago; and it is only the serious student of history who realizes the important part the fisheries played in the early history of New England, and especially of Massachusetts. "They were to us what wool was to England or tobacco to Virginia, — the great staple which became the basis of power and wealth," says Adams. Many a colossal fortune rested for its foundation upon the cod fisheries of the Banks and of Massachusetts Bay; the "codfish aristocracy" preceded both the "merchant princes" and the "lords of the loom." Even before Lexington and Concord the fervid Irish eloquence of Edmund Burke apostrophized and idealized the fisheries of the colonies. Speaking of the "wealth which the colonies have drawn from the sea by their fisheries," a wealth which he further declared had excited the envy of the British Commons, he exclaimed: "Pray, sir, what in the world is equal to it? Pass by the other parts, and look at the manner in which the people of New England have of late carried on their fisheries. Whilst we follow them among the tumbling mountains of ice and behold them penetrating into the deepest recesses of Hudson's Bay and Davis Straits, whilst we are looking for them beneath the Arctic circle, we hear that they

have pierced into the opposite region of polar cold,
that they are at the antipodes, and engaged under the
frozen serpent of the South. . . . We know that while
some of them draw the line and strike the harpoon on
the coast of Africa, others run the longitude and pur-
sue their gigantic game along the coast of Brazil. No
sea but what is vexed by their fisheries, no climate
that is not witness to their toils. Neither the perse-
verance of Holland, nor the activity of France, nor the
dexterous and firm sagacity of English enterprise, ever
carried this most perilous mode of hardy industry to
the extent to which it has been pushed by this recent
people, — a people who are still, as it were, but in the
gristle, and not yet hardened into the bone of man-
hood." So spoke Burke in the British House of Commons in March, 1775. Never before or since was
such incomparable tribute paid to those sailor pioneers,
who, springing from the rocks of Cape Cod and the
sand dunes of Nantucket, carried, in a later day, the
flag of Young America and the glory of her name to
the remotest recesses of the oceans of the globe.

An essential chapter in the history of any people
is the record of the sources from which their suste-
nance has come and from which their wealth has been
derived. Whatever may have been the inclination or
training of the hardy Englishmen who first settled on
Cape Cod, the insular position of this new coast rendered maritime pursuits necessary. When a log hut
had fortified them against the east winds of the harsh
Atlantic, and the virgin soil had yielded from its

rugged bosom the corn that was the bread of life, they turned to the immense marine preserves which lay at their very doors, and whose beckoning billows lured them to try the hazard of a hook and line. Then, as their intercourse with the Dutch along the Hudson and Long Island Sound became more thoroughly established, the tendency was to give more of their attention to the various branches of fishing, and by an exchange of products they found it less necessary to cultivate an unfriendly soil; so the trend of affairs was steadily toward those maritime pursuits which for more than two centuries since have been the characteristic and pride of Cape Cod and Cape Ann. The love of adventure is hereditary, and, if the fathers caught codfish on the Grand Banks, the sons were satisfied with nothing else than taking whales in the Pacific.

The first product of American industry exported from Massachusetts was a cargo of fish. Even the neighboring colony at Plymouth seems at first to have depended upon Cape Ann for a supply of fish. "Though famine threatened, they could not at once relieve themselves by resorting to the Bay," for their patrons in London had neglected as yet to provide for such pursuits. Once, when men staggered, says Winslow, "by reason of faintness for want of food," they were saved from famishing by the benevolence of fishermen off the coasts. Simultaneously with the settlement of Massachusetts began the despatching of cargoes of dried codfish to every country of Western Europe, as well as to the other American colonies. As early as 1634 a

merchant of the country was fishing with eight boats
at Marblehead. The next year Portsmouth had in the
fishing trade six great shallops, five fishing boats with
sails, anchors and cables, and thirteen skiffs. Of the
total product of this branch of industry in any one
year the only information is derived from Governor
Winthrop, who says that in 1641 it was followed so
well that three hundred thousand dry fish were sent
to market. Two years previously the General Court
began to recognize the importance of the industry, for
on May 22, 1639, it passed an act exempting from all
duties and public taxes all estates employed in catch-
ing, making and transporting fish, while, under the
same act, all fishermen during the season for business
and all shipbuilders were excused from training.

Between 1710 and 1750 began the active pursuit of
the maritime business by the people of Cape Cod and
Cape Ann. In 1741 about seventy fishing vessels
belonged to Gloucester. Capt. Francis Goelet, writing
of a visit to Salem in 1750, tells us that " the trade
consists chiefly of the Cod Fishery; they have sixty
or seventy sail schooners employed in the branch.
They cure all their own cod." Speaking of Marblehead, he says : " This place is noted for children and
Noureches the most of any Place for its Bigness in
North America. It is Said that the Chief Cause is
attributed to their feeding on Cod's Heads which is
their Principal Diett."

The following twenty years were full of discourage-
ments, for the wars between France and England

occasioned great annoyance, on account of the capture of vessels by the warring cruisers. The demand for men for the provincial army and navy drew heavily from the fisher population, but fishing was still pursued; in fact, it had then become the basis of a profitable coastwise and foreign trade, for the maintenance of which the merchants of the Massachusetts seaport towns would willingly encounter great risks and could afford to bear considerable losses.

In 1750 Gloucester had eighty large fishing vessels. These were sent to the Banks during the summer, and in the winter the fares of fish, together with the produce from the farms of the adjacent towns, were despatched to the West Indies, where the cargoes met a remunerative market. It is interesting to notice the causes which contributed to this profitable commerce.

The British, Spanish and French had large possessions in the West Indies. It was the policy of the home government to restrict the dealings with these colonies by passing stringent laws compelling the inhabitants to trade exclusively with the mother country. Prior to the Revolution, New England merchants, being subjects of Great Britain, had unrestricted trade with the British West Indies. Notwithstanding the rigid non-intercourse laws of the French and Spanish, illicit voyages were often made to the West Indian ports of those governments. In fact, there was an enormous smuggling trade carried on at that period. At times the pressing need of supplies obliged these governments to suspend the provisions of their prohibitive laws, and

the governors were given discretionary powers to allow
the vessels of the North Atlantic colonies licenses to
trade, discharge cargo and repair.

Most of the New England ports participated in this
trade, which was begun by the cod-fishing vessels. A
general cargo of fish, produce and live stock could be
sold in the English islands for money. The vessel
would then go to Trinidad or the Dutch possessions,
buy molasses, spices and coffee at low prices, and
return home with the cargo and quite an amount of
ready money besides; while to Europe little was sent
except the fish, the proceeds of which came back in
salt, fruit, wine and specie. This commerce was the
direct outgrowth of the fisheries.

Soon the revolutionary crisis approached, and commerce and fishery could be no longer pursued. A
great majority of the people, comprising the merchants,
mechanics, fishermen and sailors, who depended upon
the maritime business for their livelihood, could find
no employment in their regular vocations, and joined
the land or naval forces of the colonies. At the close
of the great struggle instructions were given by some
of the towns to their Representatives touching "the
importance of a restoration of the fisheries in any
arrangement that might be for peace," and requesting
them "to ask of the Legislature to see that the commissioners be instructed to that effect." This whole
question is so well set forth by a distinguished son of
Massachusetts, Mr. Charles Francis Adams, in a recent
article on "What the Codfish stands for," that the

committee are impelled to quote Mr. Adams for the benefit and instruction of the reader.

"In the winter and spring of 1779," says Mr. Adams, "the terms of a possible peace between Great Britain and her former colonies became matter for discussion in the Continental Congress. At once the question of the fisheries, and the right of Massachusetts men to participate in them, came to the front. Public law on this point had not yet been settled, for it was still the period of the close seas; and, at the beginning of the war of independence, New England had by act of Parliament been debarred from fishing on the banks of Newfoundland. Were those banks free to all nations, or would they at the restoration of peace be subject to the right of legislation by the great sea-power? France, the ally of the rebellious colonies, took the ground that the fishery of the high seas was of common right, but that the coast fisheries belonged to the proprietary of the coast; and consequently that the Massachusetts men, who had hitherto almost exclusively engaged in the fisheries of Nova Scotia and the gulf of St. Lawrence, and deemed themselves to have gained a prescriptive right in them, had in fact no right in them at all. Then followed a long legislative struggle, in which New England was for the first time arrayed against the South, and it was charged that the interests of nine of the States were being systematically sacrificed 'to gratify the eaters and distillers of molasses' in the other four. The issue was whether the right to the fisheries was to be preserved as an

ultimatum in the proposed negotiations for peace.
Through the stubborn tenacity of Samuel Adams and
Elbridge Gerry, representing Massachusetts, provision
was made that the fisheries could not be surrendered
without her consent.

"The negotiations took place in Paris, and there
John Adams represented New England interests. In
writing to him in September, 1778, Ralph Izard of
North Carolina had said, 'The fishery of Newfoundland
appears to me to be a mine of infinitely greater value
than Mexico and Peru;' and in reply to him Mr. Adams
explained why it was so; one portion of the dried fish
of Massachusetts went to the West India Islands in
exchange for rum, molasses and other West Indian
products; another portion went to the Catholic countries of Europe in exchange for gold and silver; while,
'as a nursery of seamen and a source of naval power,'
the fishery, Mr. Adams went on to say, 'has been,
and is . . . indispensably necessary to the accomplish-
ment and the preservation of our independence.' Later
in life he described how the fisheries during these
negotiations lay 'with great weight on my mind,' and
spoke of his constant apprehension lest England, in
negotiating the peace, should 'exert all her art to
deprive us of any share in that great source of wealth,
that great instrument of commerce, that great nursery
of seamen, that great means of power.' So, he said,
he lost no occasion to urge on the French representatives the general principle of the right of all nations
to the ocean and its inhabitants; while for Massachu-

setts he claimed that, so far as the fisheries were con-
cerned, ' we were in possession, and had been so, from
the first settlement of our country ; we had carried on
the fisheries from the beginning ; that the fisheries were
an essential link in the chain of American commerce,
which was one connected system.'

" When at last, in October and November, 1782,
negotiations went on in earnest, they turned on three
fundamental issues, — the boundary line, the recovery
of British debts and the fisheries ; and of these the
fisheries was the most difficult to adjust. Franklin
and Jay, the two other commissioners on the ground,
had on this point been tenacious, but they had not
made it a vital element of the proposed treaty. Mr.
Adams assumed the responsibility of declaring that the
right of fishery was indispensable to the durability of
any compact. The British negotiators asked for time
in which to obtain further instructions ; and when,
nearly three weeks later, they returned from London,
while ready to make the desired concessions in the
matter of boundaries, they would not yield the fisheries ; upon this the struggle came. ' Great Britain was
willing to concede the use on the high seas as a privilege, whilst she denied it altogether within its three
miles' jurisdiction on the coasts. The American negotiators, on the other hand, claimed the former as a right,
and asked for the privilege of the latter. Here was
the place at which Mr. Adams assumed the greatest
share of responsibility in the negotiation.' He insisted
upon placing the two countries exactly on a level in the

matter of right. Wearied with discussion, the British plenipotentiaries finally proposed to sign the preliminaries, leaving the use of terms in relation to the fishery to be adjusted when the definite treaty was framed. But even this Mr. Adams would not agree to; and, rising, he vehemently declared that, when first commissioned as a negotiator with Great Britain, his country had ordered him to make no peace without a clear acknowledgment of the right to the fishery, and by that direction he would stand. He did stand by it; and he had his way. After a short consultation among themselves the British commissioners announced their acceptance of Mr. Adams' article as he had submitted it. 'Such a victory is not often recorded in the annals of diplomacy.' It was the victory of a Massachusetts man, to whom had been confided the care of Massachusetts interests.

"This occurred on the 19th of November, 1782, and it was on the 17th of March, 1784, less than sixteen months later, that John Rowe, a member from Boston, moved permission to hang the historic codfish in the Representatives' chamber. It commemorated a diplomatic victory no less than it typified a material interest."

For more than thirty years that followed, the New England fishermen were happy. With renewed zeal they pursued their vocations, until the United States was again involved in war with Great Britain. It was well known that the mother country had never been reconciled to the fishery concessions extorted from her in the negotiations of 1783; and "again the codfish rose to the surface." Let Mr. Adams tell the story: —

"In October, 1814, the American commissioners to treat for peace sent home from Ghent the proffered British terms. They included cession of territory by the United States, the exclusion of the United States from military or naval contact with the great lakes, and the forfeiture of their rights in the fisheries. Had these terms been conceded, Massachusetts would have had sufficient grounds silently to remove the codfish from where it hung suspended from the ceiling of its Representatives' chamber.

"John Adams was then living in retirement at Quincy, but his son, John Quincy Adams, occupied at Ghent the place his father had thirty-two years before occupied at Paris. It had devolved upon him to look to it that the codfish sustained no detriment. It was on the 10th of October that the demands of Great Britain — cession of territory, abandonment of the lakes, relinquishment of the fisheries, etc. — were made known to Congress. Less than two months before, Washington had been captured by British forces, and the capitol and the White House burned. The outlook was not encouraging. Remitting to President Madison a letter received from his son, then at Ghent, John Adams thus expressed himself in the midst of that time of gloom. The date was November 28: 'All I can say is, that I would continue this war forever rather than surrender one acre of our territory, one iota of the fisheries, as established by the third article of the treaty of 1783, or one sailor impressed from any merchant ship. I will not, however, say this to my son, though I shall be very much obliged to you if you will give him orders to the same effect.'

"Incredible as it now seems, the governor of Massachusetts considered the terms of peace offered by Great Britain as favorable to America, and declared that the people of Cape Ann expected to lose the fisheries, but were willing to cede territory, if, at that price, they could retain them. The danger was imminent that the codfish would have to come down. The question was of holding the ground gained in 1783. 'In 1814, as in 1783, John Adams clung to his trophies, and his son would have waged indefinite war rather than break his father's heart by sacrificing what he had won; but at Ghent the son stood in isolation, which the father in the worst times had never known. Massachusetts left him to struggle alone for a principle that needed not only argument, but force, to make it victorious. The difficulty which Mr. Adams could not overcome arose from the fact that the treaty of 1783 not only recognized the American right to the fisheries, but it also recognized the British right to the navigation of the Mississippi. The two went together. Henry Clay was one of the commissioners at Ghent, side by side with J. Q. Adams. Clay would consent to nothing which revived the British right of navigation in the Mississippi; and so Adams found himself cut off from his appeal to the treaty of 1783 as an instrument recognizing and forever establishing mutual indefeasible rights. But, if Clay would put his name to no treaty which ceded a right of navigating the Mississippi, Adams was equally immovable in the matter of any relinquishment of the fisheries. This last the British plenipotentiaries insisted upon almost to the length of making it an ultimatum. Finally, as in 1783, they yielded the point under instructions from London, but demanded for so doing the compensatory right of navigating the Mississippi. Though Adams was now satisfied, Clay was implacable. The British then offered to make both matters subject for future negotiation; but this implied that the fishery rights secured by the treaty of 1783 were forfeited, or subject to forfeiture, — an admission Adams refused to make. And now he found himself alone, — one otherwise-minded man in five. The fishery seemed lost. Then Albert Gallatin came to the front with one last ingenious proposition, in the form of ʻa note rejecting the British stipulation, because it implied the abandonment of a right, but offering to be silent as to both the fisheries and the Mississippi, or to admit a general reference to further negotiation of all subjects in dispute, so expressed as to imply no abandonment of right.ʼ

"And this was the famous treaty of Ghent! The younger Adams had not succeeded in saving all of those expressed and extraordinary rights which the elder Adams had won; but, preserving those rights from formal and absolute relinquishment, he secured a result not less practically valuable than that achieved by his father, by causing the reference of all the

points at issue to be settled by time and the course
of events, those final arbitrators, in whose decision, as
the event proved, he could safely trust."

And, as Mr. Adams says in his closing paragraph,
of all this is the codfish in the Representatives' hall
emblematic; "it tells of commerce, war, diplomacy;
of victories won by Massachusetts in all three fields."

CHAPTER III.

Years before the statesmen of the period had decided
to make public acknowledgment of the indebtedness of
the colony to the codfish, and had voted to adorn the
assembly chamber with a wooden representation thereof,
individuals and private corporations were eager to pay
tribute to the codfish, and vied with one another in
their anxiety to make the recognition as conspicuous
as possible. As early as 1661 the codfish appears upon
the corporate seal of the Plymouth Land Company,
proprietors of lands on the Kennebec River. In 1743
Col. Benjamin Pickman of Salem, who was one of the
most prominent men of the colony, erected the Mansion
House in that town, and decorated the end of every
stair in his spacious hall with a carved and gilded codfish. Some of the journals of the day recognized it.
On the front of the "Salem Gazette" for 1768 appears
a coat of arms, consisting of a shield, supported by two
Indians, and bearing the dove and olive branch. The
crest above this shield is an unmistakable codfish.

Official notice of the obligation owed to the people

of the colony had been taken, and the emblem inserted in some of the court seals, among others, upon the seal affixed to the processes issued from the famous Court of Oyer and Terminer, which tried and condemned the witches in 1692. The origin of the seal seems to have been traced as far back as 1686, when it was used by the Court of Quarter Sessions of the Peace and the Inferior Court of Common Pleas, as well as in the melancholy instances referred to above. The seal bears the word "Essex," elegantly carved in cipher, with what passes for the dove and olive branch above it, and an unmistakable codfish below.

Again, the seal of the "Middle Circuit Court of Common Pleas" shows the codfish. In the margin of the seal is the word "Massachusetts," with the style of court, and on its face "Fiat Justitia," under which motto agriculture, commerce and the fisheries are respectively represented by the sheep, the anchor and the codfish. This court was established in 1811, by an act dividing the Commonwealth into six circuits, each having a chief justice and associates. The "Middle Circuit" comprised Essex, Middlesex and Suffolk.

The Commonwealth paid tribute to this source of her earliest prosperity in other directions. In 1755 a two-penny internal revenue stamp of the colony bore the impress of the codfish, surrounded with this striking and significant legend: "Staple of the Massachusetts." This stamp may be seen, says Felt, upon a contract for building the draw of the old North bridge at Salem, which draw, being raised at the approach of

Leslie's Regulars, twenty years later, became the bulwark of the liberties of America.

The currency of the colony at a later date bore the same impress on several of its issues. In the years 1776 and 1778 many of the coins, from three-pence upwards, seem to have been thus embellished. In an old collection of American currency the following denominations bear the tutelary fish upon their face: In 1776, $3, $5, $8, $11, also 3d, 6d, 8d, 9d, 1s, 1s 6d, 2s, 3s, 4s and 4s 6d; in 1778, 4d, 1s 6d, 2s, 3s, 4s and 4s 6d.

Thus it appears that the use of the codfish as a symbol of the progress and pre-eminence of Massachusetts was no novel or unaccustomed departure. The homely emblem is closely identified with the greatness of the State. It might almost be said that its crescent outlines are graven on every page of its history.

Tradition invests our codfish with the grandeur gathered from the days when "there were giants" in Massachusetts. It speaks to us of all the old Bay State was and is. Patriotism protects it from the cavil of the cynic and the gibe of the unthinking. It typifies the world-old simplicity of those who go down to the sea in ships; the goodly, Godly race, whom the stately scriptural story has immortalized; whose sturdy virtues the Saviour himself distinguished in the choice of Peter, the apostolic fisherman; and whose singular achievements on sea and land, in the arts alike of peace and war, have glorified the annals of the Commonwealth.

Representatives' Chamber, Bulfinch State House.

ADDRESS

OF

REPRESENTATIVE IRWIN.

The foregoing report being under consideration, Representative Richard W. Irwin of Northampton addressed the House as follows: —

MR. SPEAKER: — I rise to ask you to place in the
new House of Representatives, as it was in the old,
the emblem of the codfish. I do not purpose to tell
you of its long history, or of the patriotic hands which
won for us our liberty and gave a continent to freedom, which placed it there. I pray that we, who put
it in its new position, may be as fervent in our
patriotism and love of liberty and right, as brave to
act and as willing to suffer, as those who, over a
century ago, hung it high in yonder hall.

But I rise to call to your attention, their successors
in unbroken line and heirs of their great gift, some
things this emblem means and teaches: what it tells
of those sufferings which a nation must endure ere it
have the courage, fortitude and strength of greatness;
somewhat of the humble heroes, bred in the fisheries,
whom it calls to mind; some of the ancient glories of

our Commonwealth, which, though the symbol be plain
and lowly, come back to mind at its sight. Is it ,
plain and humble? It has always been so of emblems
that tell of deeds and purposes really great. Such
emblems speak the thought of the common people,
which is not delicate or poetic, but simple and plain,
needing no interpreter.

Whence came the term "Puritan" but from a word
of derision, adopted afterwards in honor and pride?
Whence the song of "Yankee Doodle," to whose tune
Burgoyne laid down his arms at Saratoga and Corn-
wallis at Yorktown? What song but that of "John
Brown's body," born on the march from soldiers'
thought, led our country on through the long and
flaming way to the freedom of the slave and a nation's
regeneration? The rugged bear has for years represented the strength of the Russians. The symbol of
the bee told of the great Napoleon. England's chan-
cellors for hundreds of years have sat upon the wool-
sack in front of the throne. The rose and the simple
cross of St. George tell the story of England's morn-
ing drum-beat. It was under the lilies of France that
men followed the plume of Navarre. In all ages of
the Church the brazen serpent has been the emblem
of Christianity, and the cross upon which our Saviour
suffered has been the symbol under and before which a
whole world worships.

The plain codfish has, too, its own story. More
than the Indian upon our State seal, it is the proper
emblem of Massachusetts. It tells the story of struggle

and privations of Pilgrim and Puritan, whom many
times it relieved in want and famine; of commerce that
brought golden returns, and made our colony rich; of
fleets that whitened the waters of many and far-off seas.
It tells of victories that Massachusetts won in diplomacy, no less renowned than war's; of the treaties of
Paris and Ghent, where some of our greatest sons,
Gerry and the elder and younger Adams, matched
against the diplomats of England, trained by contest
with Napoleon and Talleyrand, overcame and discom-
fited them. You properly carve their names upon the
walls of this house, in that chaplet of worthies which
is the Cornelian crown of jewels of our State. Shall
you leave outside the emblem of those fisheries for
which they fought? It calls to mind the seamen who,
enured to hardship, made bold and daring by their
daily struggle with the defiant and threatening seas,
learned in those same fisheries strength, courage and
seamanship, such as, else, the world has never seen.

This nation's proudest glory is a story of war by
sea, and Massachusetts has no greater honor than that
her seamen stood upon the ships and manned the
frigates by which those memorable and renowned victories were won. For it was with the fishermen of
the capes and banks that Paul Jones drove before him,
like petrels before the storm, the captains who fought
under Nelson at Trafalgar. It was these seamen who
went with Decatur up the harbor of Tripoli. It was
our own Isaac Hull before whose flaming guns the
"Guerriere" went down. These men manned the guns

of the "Constitution" and the "President." They brought back the dead body of Lawrence up yonder harbor, wrapped in his country's flag; and in a war, which else had ended in disaster, they taught England that her daughter was an empress of the sea.

Nor was their patriotism or valor confined to the seas which were their home. The little fishing town of Marblehead alone sent a whole regiment to the war of the Revolution; and there stands upon Commonwealth Avenue in this great city, whose wealth came largely from the cod fisheries, a statue telling how General Glover of Marblehead and his men carried Washington and his army across the almost impassable Delaware, in that awful night, and thus saved the Continental army, its immortal leader and its glorious cause.

This incident was related to this House a few years later by General Knox, when, as a member from Marblehead, he pleaded that his constituents might have the right to do banking. He rose and stated their claim. "I am surprised," he said, "that Marblehead should ask so small a privilege as that of banking, and that there should be any opposition to it. Sir, I wish the members of this body knew the people of Marblehead as well as I do. I could wish that they stood on the Delaware River in 1776, in that bitter night when the Commander-in-Chief had drawn up his little army to cross it, and had seen the powerful current bearing onward the floating masses of ice which threatened destruction to whosoever should venture upon its bosom. I wish that when this occurrence threatened to defeat the enterprise they could have heard that distinguished warrior demand, 'Who will lead us on?' and seen the men of Marblehead, and Marblehead alone, stand forward to lead the army along the perilous paths to unfading glories and honors in the achievements of Trenton. There, sir, went the fishermen of Marblehead, alike at home upon land or water, alike ardent, patriotic and unflinching, wherever they unfurled the flag of their country."

That plain codfish shall ever call to mind the humble calling which made these men able, adventurous, firm and strong. Their memory rises to-day, — sad memory of cruel death by storm and wave, proud and glorious memory of death in victorious battle, — and pleads with us that the emblem of the fisheries in which they were made and developed to be a nation's bulwark and a nation's arm of power may not be discarded and rejected as unworthy of the gilded glories of this House. They were men from our own coast and harbors. They were your sons, — Gloucester, gray Marblehead and wind-scourged Essex. Nay, more, they were your sons, O proud and beautiful, our mother State. Their hazards and brave deeds were for your renown; their sufferings and death were for your glory. Many of their names are graven on this your temple. Your voice has already spoken throughout your borders, bidding that the emblem that tells of them shall be placed before your altar. May that voice be heeded by this House to-day.

This emblem speaks in vibrant tones of danger met and glorious victories won. It tells also of the world-old but yearly recurring and never-ending story of the sorrow and tragedy of the sea. We think as we look upon it of the death that lives in the fogs and ice of Newfoundland and in the mighty power of the tempest and plunging waters. We hear the yearly uttered cry of sorrow and of anguish from Marblehead and Gloucester, when the fleet comes back bringing its pitiful story of accident and death. It tells us of the remorseless sea that kills, and buries not its dead; of the young and strong that are torn from life by crushing ice and ravenous waves; of the widow and her clinging orphans set face to face with poverty; of eyes that weep uncomforted; of hearts that break and never mend. It is a story that fish has told for over a hundred years, and will tell again as long as men go down to the sea in ships to win from its alluring and treacherous tide a living for those they love.

For over a century that symbol has hung in the House of Representatives, — for over a century, in which Massachusetts has won her proud pre-eminence among the States. It has witnessed there the passage of all the wise and beneficent laws that have made us a model Commonwealth, — laws which relieve the poor and ignorant, which help those who labor, which made education the Ægis of our government and made elections pure and free; which did equity and justice, and made for progress in step with the advancing years. It saw Massachusetts lead, as she still leads, the pro-

cession of the States with the commanding step of
conscious and conceded leadership. For, —

> " Wise men at her council met,
> Who knew the seasons when to take
> Occasion by the hand, and make
> The bounds of freedom wider yet,
> By shaping some august decree,
> Broad based upon the people's will."

It saw there Lafayette, Kossuth and the determined
and silent Grant. It has seen most of our governors
inaugurated with formal pomp and state. It heard
Webster, Choate and Shaw, as they discussed the Constitution of the Commonwealth. It heard the matchless
voice of Phillips, as he pleaded for the freedom of the
slave and demanded the impeachment of the unjust
judge. It may have heard Andrew, as he prayed in
his room at midnight that his country might be spared;
and again, after the sad years, in the council-room
which it faces, singing, when the news came that
Vicksburg had fallen and Gettysburg was won, the old
doxology of thanksgiving. It has heard coming up
the windows, as they passed by the State House, the
cheering shouts, the playing bands and the martial
tread of marching men, as Massachusetts through four
long years sent forth her chosen, her bravest and her
tenderest to freedom's war. It knew when Bartlett of
Pittsfield went by at the head of his regiment, — the
man in whom Sidney lived, fought and died again; it
heard the solemn, determined step of the colored regi-

ment which Robert Shaw led on, in hopeless charge,
to death at Fort Wagner. It saw the Massachusetts
dead brought tenderly back from Baltimore, the State's
first sacrifice upon the bloody altar of war. And then,
when the war was over, and a nation builded anew, it
saw that glad home-coming when the battle-flags came
back; when up the streets and past the cheering thou-
sands, and through the wide gates of the capitol, came
the regiments thin and shattered and wounded, bearing
their shot and crimsoned flags of war, and moving in
a cloud of glory which time shall never dim: —

> "Blest, and thrice blest the Roman,
>   Who sees Rome's brightest day,
> Who sees that long, victorious pomp
>   Wind down the Sacred Way!
> And through the bellowing Forum,
>   And round the suppliant's Grove,
> Up to the everlasting gates
>   Of Capitolian Jove."

Is this emblem said to be too common and plain to
accord with the painted splendors of this place? It is
no more common, simple and plain than the fathers
who founded our State. It tells how the lowliest may
rise and win and rule; how the fisherman may be the
peer of the marshals of France and the admirals of
England. Are there those who laugh at it? It speaks
of pathetic deaths for many years in lowly but honorable livelihood. Do you say it is unimportant? The
ablest of statesmen have contended about it at the

council of kings. Do you cavil or deride it? It tells you of victories on sea and land which history crowns with lustrous and unfading glory, which our proud State tells over as among her priceless jewels, which children and children yet unborn shall learn and tell to others with heightening cheeks and brightened eyes.

Let us never say — we, sons of the weaver, the carpenter and the fisherman — that the day of small things is to be despised; that the lowly and plain condition of our fathers is to be forgotten, or that anything for which they cared or which they preferred is not worthy of us. Let us take it in reverence and honor, and place it on high as one of the proudest decorations of this great hall; and let it remain there so long as this State House shall stand, a memorial of the Pilgrim, his privations and simplicity; an emblem significant of the hardiness, courage and faith of those who dare and defy the seas, and daily telling of the great and surpassing glories of Massachusetts and her sons.

New Representatives' Chamber.

APPENDIX.

LIST OF MEMBERS

OF THE

Executive Council, the Senate and House of Representatives.

GOVERNOR AND COUNCIL.

FREDERIC T. GREENHALGE OF LOWELL,
GOVERNOR.

HIS HONOR

ROGER WOLCOTT OF BOSTON,
LIEUTENANT GOVERNOR.

COUNCILLORS.

District I.

ZIBA C. KEITH . . . of Brockton.

District II.

CYRUS SAVAGE . . . . of Taunton.

District III.

FRANCIS H. RAYMOND . . . of Somerville.

District IV.

JOHN H. SULLIVAN . . of Boston.

District V.

B. FRANK SOUTHWICK . . of Peabody.

District VI.

JOHN M. HARLOW . . . of Woburn.

District VII.

CHARLES E. STEVENS . . . of Ware.

District VIII.

ALVAN BARRUS . . of Goshen.

SENATE.

PRESIDENT:

Hon. WILLIAM M. BUTLER, . . New Bedford.

NAME.	ADDRESS.	DISTRICT.
Atherton, Horace H., . .	Saugus, . .	Fifth Essex.
Atwood, Edward B., . . .	Plymouth, . .	First Plymouth.
Bessom, Eugene A., ...	Lynn, . . .	First Essex.
Bill, Ledyard, ...	Paxton, . .	Third Worcester.
Blodgett, Percival, ...	Templeton, .	{ Worcester and Hampshire. }
Bradford, Edward S., . . .	Springfield, . .	First Hampden.
Burns, George J., ...	Ayer, . . .	Fifth Middlesex.
Butler, William M., ...	New Bedford, .	Third Bristol.
Corbett, Joseph J., ...	Boston, . . .	Second Suffolk.
Darling, Francis W., . . .	Hyde Park, . .	First Norfolk.
Durant, William B., ...	Cambridge, . .	Third Middlesex.
Foss, Ether S., ...	Lowell, . . .	Seventh Middlesex.
Frothingham, Edward G., . .	Haverhill, . .	Fourth Essex.
Fuller, Granville A., . . .	Boston, . . .	Eighth Suffolk.
Gage, George L., ...	Lawrence, . .	Sixth Essex.

SENATE – Concluded.

NAME.			ADDRESS.		DISTRICT.
Galloupe, George A.,	.	.	Beverly,	. .	Second Essex.
Gilbride, Michael B.,	. .	.	Boston, .	.	Third Suffolk.
Gray, Robert S.,	. .	.	Walpole,	. .	Second Norfolk.
Harvey, Edwin B.,* .	. .	.	Westborough,	.	Second Worcester.
Hutchinson, Isaac P.,	. .	.	Boston, . .	.	Seventh Suffolk.
Lawrence, George P.,	. .	.	North Adams,	.	Berkshire.
Leach, James C.,	. .	.	Bridgewater,	.	Second Plymouth.
Maccabe, Joseph B., .	. .	.	Boston, . .	.	First Suffolk.
Malone, Dana, .	. .	.	Greenfield,	. .	Franklin.
McMorrow, William H., .	. .		Boston, . .	.	Sixth Suffolk.
Miller, Joel D., .	. .		Leominster, .	.	Fourth Worcester.
Morse, William A., .	. .		Tisbury,	. .	Cape.
Neill, Joseph O.,	. .	.	Fall River, .	.	Second Bristol.
Niles, James P.,†	. .	.	Watertown, .	.	Second Middlesex.
Perkins, George W., .	. .	.	Somerville, .	.	First Middlesex.
Quinn, John, Jr.,	. .	.	Boston, .	.	Fourth Suffolk.
Reed, George A.,	. .	.	Framingham,	.	Fourth Middlesex.
Ripley, John B.,	. .	.	Chester,		{ Berkshire and Hampshire. }
Salisbury, Stephen, .	. .	.	Worcester,	. .	First Worcester.
Sanger, George P., .	. .	.	Boston, .	.	Fifth Suffolk.
Smith, Sylvanus,	. .	.	Gloucester,	. .	Third Essex.
Southard, Louis C., .	. .		Easton, .	.	First Bristol.
Sprague, Charles F., .	. .	.	Boston, . .	.	Ninth Suffolk.
Wellman, Arthur H.,	. .	.	Malden,	.	Sixth Middlesex.
Whitcomb, Marciene H., .	. .		Holyoke,	. .	Second Hampden.

* Resigned June 5, 1895.
† Elected Feb. 26, 1895, to fill vacancy caused by death of Oliver Shaw, Senator-elect.

GEORGE V. L. MEYER.
Speaker, 1894 —

HOUSE OF REPRESENTATIVES.

SPEAKER:

Hon. GEORGE v. L. MEYER,   .   .   .   Boston.

NAME.	DISTRICT.	ADDRESS.
Allen, Daniel W., . . .	19, Essex, . .	Lynn.
Allen, Romeo E., . . .	12, Worcester .	Shrewsbury.
Atsatt, Isaiah P., ...	7, Plymouth, .	Mattapoisett.
Austin, Frederick E., . . .	3, Bristol, . .	Taunton.
Bailey, George W., . . .	4, Berkshire, .	Pittsfield.
Bailey, James A., Jr., . . .	15, Middlesex, .	Arlington.
Baker, Theophilus B., . . .	2, Barnstable, .	Harwich.
Balch, Charles T., ...	7, Essex, . .	Groveland.
Bancroft, Charles G., . . .	13, Worcester, .	Clinton.
Bancroft, Solon, ...	14, Middlesex, .	Reading.
Barber, Harding R., . . .	1, Worcester, .	Athol.
Barker, Albert F., . . .	3, Plymouth, .	Hanson.
Barnes, Erwin F., . . .	6, Berkshire, .	West Stockbridge.
Barnes, Franklin O., . . .	26, Suffolk, . .	Chelsea.

HOUSE OF REPRESENTATIVES – CONTINUED.

NAME.	DISTRICT.	ADDRESS.
Barry, Daniel J.,	14, Suffolk,	Boston.
Bates, John L.,	1, Suffolk,	Boston.
Beaman, Algernon T.,	4, Worcester,	Princeton.
Bennett, Frank S.,*	24, Middlesex,	Tyngsborough.
Bird, George B.,	24, Suffolk,	Boston.
Bliss, Henry C.,	2, Hampden,	West Springfield.
Blodgett, Benjamin F.,	5, Worcester,	West Brookfield.
Bond, Charles P.,	18, Middlesex,	Waltham.
Bourne, Samuel S.,	8, Plymouth,	Middleborough.
Boutwell, Harvey L.,	9, Middlesex,	Malden.
Bradford, Fred. H.,	18, Middlesex,	Waltham.
Bradley, Manassah E.,	2, Suffolk,	Boston.
Brown, Charles D.,	10, Essex,	Gloucester.
Brown, Frederick A.,	8, Worcester,	Webster.
Bullock, Benjamin S.,	10, Essex,	Manchester.
Burges, William H.,†	2, Plymouth,	Kingston.
Burt, J. Marshall,	9, Hampden,	East Longmeadow.
Burt, T. Preston,	3, Bristol,	Taunton.
Carroll, Charles W.,	11, Worcester,	Milford.
Carter, William,	9, Norfolk,	Needham.
Casey, Daniel C.,	20, Suffolk,	Boston.
Chandler, Frank,	16, Middlesex,	Belmont.
Clark, Luther W.,	4, Franklin,	Deerfield.
Cochran, James A.,	1, Suffolk,	Boston.
Collins, Michael W.,	3, Suffolk,	Boston.
Cook, Heman S.,	3, Barnstable,	Provincetown.
Cook, Gilbert,‡	14, Worcester,	Lunenburg.

* Died April 10.   † Died June 5.   ‡ Died February 17.

HOUSE OF REPRESENTATIVES – CONTINUED.

NAME.	DISTRICT.	ADDRESS.
Creed, James F., . . .	15, Suffolk, . .	Boston.
Crane, Ellery B.,*	21, Worcester, .	Worcester.
Dallinger, Frederick W., . . .	2, Middlesex, .	Cambridge.
Davis, William W., ...	21, Suffolk, . .	Boston.
Denham, Thomas M., . . .	5, Bristol, . .	New Bedford.
Dickinson, David T., . . .	1, Middlesex, .	Cambridge.
Donahue, Thomas, ...	8, Bristol, . .	Fall River.
Donovan, Timothy J., . . .	4, Suffolk, . .	Boston.
Donovan, William F., . . .	8, Suffolk, . .	Boston.
Donovan, William J., . . .	2, Suffolk, . .	Boston.
Dow, Harry R., ...	5, Essex, . .	Lawrence.
Drew, William H., ...	1, Plymouth, .	Plymouth.
Driscoll, Daniel M., ...	12, Suffolk, . .	Boston.
Driscoll, William P., . . .	12, Suffolk, . .	Boston.
Drury, Levi A., ...	3, Essex, . .	Bradford.
Duddy, Robert, ...	7, Middlesex, .	Somerville.
Eddy, George M., ...	6, Bristol, . .	New Bedford.
Edgarton, Henry, ...	32, Middlesex, .	Shirley.
Edgerton, Albert H., . . .	5, Worcester, .	Sturbridge.
Eldredge, Alpheus M., . . .	11, Plymouth, .	Brockton.
Estes, Benjamin F., ...	19, Essex, . .	Lynn.
Fallon, Thomas F., ...	19, Suffolk, . .	Boston.
Ferson, Clarentine E., . . .	15, Worcester, .	Fitchburg.
Fillmore, Wellington, . . .	2, Middlesex, .	Cambridge.
Fisk, Henry H., ...	1, Barnstable, .	Dennis.
Flint, James H.,†	5, Norfolk, . .	Weymouth.
Flint, Silas W., ...	13, Middlesex, .	Wakefield.

* Elected to succeed Henry Y. Simpson, deceased.   † Resigned June 5, 1895.

HOUSE OF REPRESENTATIVES – CONTINUED.

NAME.	DISTRICT.	ADDRESS.
Flynn, Joseph J.,	4, Essex,	Lawrence.
Foote, William H.,	2, Hampden,	Westfield.
Ford, William E.,	23, Suffolk,	Boston.
Foss, Otis,	1, Dukes,	Cottage City.
Fowle, George E.,	14, Middlesex,	Woburn.
French, Zenas A.,	6, Norfolk,	Holbrook.
Gallivan, James A.,	13, Suffolk,	Boston.
Gardner, John J.,	1, Nantucket,	Nantucket.
Gauss, John D. H.,	13, Essex,	Salem.
Gaylord, Henry E.,	3, Hampshire,	South Hadley.
Geary, Michael P.,	13, Suffolk,	Boston.
George, Samuel W.,	2, Essex,	Haverhill.
Gillingham, James L.,	4, Bristol,	Fairhaven.
Goodrich, Charles W.,	3, Berkshire,	Hinsdale.
Graham, William T.,	5, Suffolk,	Boston.
Grant, Alexander,	5, Hampden,	Chicopee.
Gray, Joshua S.,	5, Plymouth,	Rockland.
Greenwood, Abner,	27, Middlesex,	Ashland.
Grover, Thomas E.,	4, Norfolk,	Canton.
Hale, Edward A.,	8, Essex,	Newburyport.
Hammond, Charles L.,	5, Norfolk,	Quincy.
Hammond, George,	7, Worcester,	Charlton.
Harlow, Franklin P.,	6, Plymouth,	Whitman.
Harrington, James L.,*	14, Worcester,	Lunenburg.
Harvey, Benjamin C.,	8, Hampden,	Springfield.
Harwood, Albert L.,	17, Middlesex,	Newton Centre.
Hastings, Samuel,	2, Franklin,	Warwick.

* Elected to succeed Gilbert Cook, deceased.

HOUSE OF REPRESENTATIVES – CONTINUED.

NAME.	DISTRICT.	ADDRESS.
Hathaway, Bowers C., . . .	12, Worcester, .	Westborough.
Hathaway, Frederic W., . . .	12, Plymouth, .	Brockton.
Hawkes, Wesley O., . . .	31, Middlesex, .	Westford.
Hayes, William H. I., .	24, Middlesex, .	Lowell.
Hibbard, George A., . .	18, Suffolk, . .	Boston.
Higgins, Sumner C., . .	4, Middlesex, .	Cambridge.
Hoban, Thomas F., . . .	25, Middlesex, .	Lowell.
Holden, Joshua B., . . .	11, Suffolk, . .	Boston.
Holland, Timothy, . .	19, Suffolk, . .	Boston.
Hollis, J. Edward, . . .	17, Middlesex, .	Newton.
Holt, E. Clarence, . .	3, Bristol, . .	Taunton.
Horan, John G., . .	15, Suffolk, . .	Boston.
Howe, Louis P., . . .	29, Middlesex, .	Marlborough.
Humphrey, Henry D., . .	1, Norfolk, . .	Dedham.
Huse, Caleb B., . . .	8, Essex, . .	Newburyport.
Hutchinson, W. Henry, . .	20, Essex, . .	Lynn.
Irwin, Richard W., . . .	1, Hampshire, .	Northampton.
Ives, Dwight H., . .	3, Hampden, .	Holyoke.
Jenks, William S., . . .	2, Berkshire, .	Adams.
Johnson, Edward P., . .	18, Essex, . .	Lynn.
Jones, George R., .	11, Middlesex, .	Melrose.
Jordan, Cyrus A., . .	14, Essex, . .	Salem.
Jourdan, Benjamin A., . . .	10, Worcester, .	Upton.
Kaan, Frank W., . . .	6, Middlesex, .	Somerville.
Keenan, James, . . .	16, Suffolk, . .	Boston.
Keenan, Thomas P., . . .	8, Suffolk, . .	Boston.
Kellogg, John E., . . .	15, Worcester, .	Fitchburg.

HOUSE OF REPRESENTATIVES—CONTINUED.

NAME.	DISTRICT.	ADDRESS.
Kimball, William G., . .	2, Hampshire, .	Huntington.
Kingman, Francis M., .	9, Plymouth, .	East Bridgewater.
Knox, Joseph B., ...	22, Worcester, .	Worcester.
Krebbs, Franz H., Jr , .	17, Suffolk, . .	Boston.
Lawrence, Amos A., . . .	4, Plymouth, .	Cohasset.
Leach, George A., . . .	28, Middlesex, .	Wayland.
Leach, Osgood L., .	3, Franklin, .	Northfield.
Leach, Warren S., . . .	2, Bristol, . .	Raynham.
Light, Charles F., . . .	3, Norfolk, . .	Hyde Park.
Lowell, Francis C., . . .	11, Suffolk, . .	Boston.
Lynch, John M., . .	4, Essex, . .	Lawrence.
Macomber, John A., 2d, . .	7, Bristol, . .	Westport.
Mann, Hugo, ...	5, Franklin, .	Buckland.
Marden, William H., . .	12, Middlesex, .	Stoneham.
Mayo, Samuel N., . . .	8, Middlesex, .	Medford.
McCarthy, Jeremiah J., . .	4, Suffolk, . .	Boston.
McMackin, Bernard, . .	7, Suffolk, . .	Boston.
Melaven, James F., . . .	20, Worcester, .	Worcester.
Mellen, George H., . . .	23, Worcester, .	Worcester.
Mellen, James H., .	19, Worcester, .	Worcester.
Meyer, George v. L., .	9, Suffolk, . .	Boston.
Mills, Charles E., .	9, Bristol, . .	Fall River.
Mitchell, Samuel H., .	25, Suffolk, . .	Boston.
Mooney, Joseph F., .	8, Bristol, . .	Fall River.
Moore, E. Lewis, .	28, Middlesex, .	Framingham.
Moran, William, .	8, Bristol, . .	Fall River.
Moriarty, Eugene M., . . .	18, Worcester, .	Worcester.

HOUSE OF REPRESENTATIVES – CONTINUED.

NAME.	DISTRICT.	ADDRESS.
Mulvey, Mark B.,	22, Suffolk,	Boston.
Murphy, Timothy F.,	7, Suffolk,	Boston.
Myers, James J.,	1, Middlesex,	Cambridge.
Newell, Herbert,	1, Franklin,	Shelburne.
Newell, Richard,	1, Essex,	West Newbury.
Newhall, George H.,	17, Essex,	Lynn.
Newhall, John B.,	18, Essex,	Lynn.
Norton, Joseph J.,	14, Suffolk,	Boston.
O'Brien, Michael J.,	5, Suffolk,	Boston.
O'Connor, John J.,	23, Middlesex,	Lowell.
O'Hara, John M.,	3, Suffolk,	Boston.
Osgood, L. Edgar,	6, Essex,	North Andover.
Parker, Theodore K.,	2, Worcester,	Winchendon.
Penniman, George W.,	10, Plymouth,	Brockton.
Perkins, Lyman H.,	6, Hampden,	Springfield.
Phelps, Carlton T.,*	1, Berkshire,	North Adams.
Pinkham, Edward W.,	17, Essex,	Lynn.
Porter, Burrill, Jr.,	1, Bristol,	No. Attleborough.
Porter, George W.,	7, Norfolk,	Avon.
Porter, J. Frank,	22, Essex,	Danvers.
Prevaux, John J.,	1, Essex,	Amesbury.
Putnam, George E.,	22, Middlesex,	Lowell.
Quint, Nicolas M.,	21, Essex,	Peabody.
Quirk, Charles I.,	20, Suffolk,	Boston.
Rice, Henry F.,	9, Worcester,	Sutton.
Richardson, Robert A.,	3, Essex,	Haverhill.
Roberts, Ernest W.,	27, Suffolk,	Chelsea.

* Resigned June 5, 1895.

HOUSE OF REPRESENTATIVES—CONTINUED.

NAME.	DISTRICT.	ADDRESS.
Roe, Alfred S., ...	16, Worcester, .	Worcester.
Root, Silas B., ...	1, Hampden, .	Granville.
Roper, George A., ...	24, Middlesex, .	Lowell.
Ross, Samuel, ...	5, Bristol, . .	New Bedford.
Rourke, Daniel D., ...	6, Suffolk, . .	Boston.
Rourke, Fred H., . . .	21, Middlesex, .	Lowell.
Russell, George G., ...	15, Essex, . .	Salem.
Ryan, James F., ...	16, Suffolk, . .	Boston.
Ryder, Martin F., ...	6, Suffolk, . .	Boston.
Sargent, Charles F., ...	5, Essex, . .	Lawrence.
Scates, George M., ...	21, Suffolk, . .	Boston.
Searls, William P., ...	17, Worcester, .	Worcester.
Shea, John T., ...	3, Middlesex, .	Cambridge.
Sheehan, John F., ...	4, Hampden, .	Holyoke.
Shepherd, William, ...	20, Essex, . .	Lynn.
Sibley, Frank M., ...	5, Hampshire, .	Ware.
Sisson, Henry D., ...	7, Berkshire, .	New Marlborough.
Slade, David F., ...	9, Bristol, . .	Fall River.
Sleeper, George T., ...	27, Suffolk, . .	Winthrop.
Smith, Albert C., ...	18, Suffolk, . .	Boston.
Smith, Henry M., ...	5, Berkshire, .	Lee.
Snow, George F., ...	20, Middlesex, .	Chelmsford.
Southworth, Amasa E., . . .	5, Middlesex, .	Somerville.
Spalding, Warren F., . . .	4, Middlesex, .	Cambridge.
Spofford, John C., ...	10, Middlesex, .	Everett.
Spring, Arthur L., ...	10, Suffolk, . .	Boston.
Stanley, Fred D., ...	6, Bristol, . .	New Bedford.

HOUSE OF REPRESENTATIVES – CONTINUED.

NAME.	DISTRICT.	ADDRESS.
Stevens, Ezra A.,	9, Middlesex,	Malden.
St. John, Thomas E.,	2, Essex,	Haverhill.
Stocker, Joseph W.,	12, Essex,	Beverly.
Stone, Daniel D.,	9, Essex,	Hamilton.
Strong, Homer O.,	1, Hampshire,	Southampton.
Sturtevant, Charles F.,	23, Suffolk,	Boston.
Tarr, George J.,	10, Essex,	Gloucester.
Teamoh, Robert T.,	9, Suffolk,	Boston.
Thacher, Josiah P.,	30, Middlesex,	Littleton.
Thurston, Lyman D.,	6, Worcester,	Leicester.
Tolman, William,	4, Berkshire,	Pittsfield.
Tower, Henry,	29, Middlesex,	Hudson.
Towle, William W.,	17, Suffolk,	Boston.
Tuite, Michael,	11, Worcester,	Blackstone.
Turner, Arthur H.,	13, Worcester,	Harvard.
Turner, George W.,*	6, Hampden,	Springfield.
Tuttle, John E.,	24, Suffolk,	Boston.
Utley, Charles H.,	2, Norfolk,	Brookline.
Wadden, Frank L.,	16, Essex,	Marblehead.
Waite, Gilman,	2, Worcester,	Templeton.
Wakefield, Charles E.,	4, Hampshire,	Amherst.
Wales, George A.,	7, Norfolk,	Stoughton.
Wallis, Horace E.,	10, Hampden,	Holland.
Warriner, Stephen C.,	8, Hampden,	Springfield.
Waterman, George B.,	1, Berkshire,	Williamstown.
Wentworth, George L.,	5, Norfolk,	Weymouth.
Weston, Clarence P.,	10, Suffolk,	Boston.

* Elected to succeed Joseph L. Shipley, deceased.

HOUSE OF REPRESENTATIVES—CONCLUDED.

NAME.	DISTRICT.	ADDRESS.
Wheaton, Mark O., . . .	1, Bristol, . .	Attleborough.
Whitaker, Elbridge J., .	8, Norfolk, . .	Wrentham.
White, George E., ...	1, Barnstable, .	Sandwich.
White, William S., ...	8, Norfolk, . .	Foxborough.
Wiley, Albert L., ...	3, Worcester, .	Hardwick.
Willard, Edward E., . . .	26, Suffolk, . .	Chelsea.
Wilson, Edward H , . . .	26, Middlesex, .	Natick.
Winn, John, . . .	19, Middlesex, .	Woburn .
Wood, Henry O., ...	10, Bristol, . .	Swanzey.
Woodfall, J. Loring, . .	11, Essex, . .	Rockport.
Young, Charles L , ...	7, Hampden, .	Springfield.

www.ingramcontent.com/pod-product-compliance
Lightning Source LLC
Chambersburg PA
CBHW071931020426
42331CB00010B/2807